# *The Rose*

## Connie Holt

Inks and Bindings
888-290-5218
www.inksandbindings.com
orders@inksandbindings.com

# Contents

# Traveler's May

Long-awaited season came
gentle kissed
May's gift flowers still damp,
from evening mist
Puffy shadowed clouds ride on
gentle breezes
Diamond shaped patch of sky
showed through the trees
One gaunt and bare, May's
air filled sweet perfume flowers,
in love's care
Traveling over claimed a season,
poured abundant rains, and
settled there
Sun will shine again
Way showing grace
May forgiveness, in its best

# Sweet Freedom's Song

Movement unseen, yet it comes,
quietly, as a soft breeze
Silently with measured steps among,
each flower, each tree
A gentle stir laughter, pearled shells
Are sounds of the season that ring,
Out through the air like a bell
Sweet words like memories, peaceful
and new
Soft, clear and kissed by morning dew
Proudly it stands beside freedom's
sweet song
Throughout filled with pink perfume,
from ransomed throng
Raindrops bejeweled trees layers, like
scarves among leaves
Soft light on dawn petals played,
upon the song
Fades, into a broken tune later on
The flowering day did sleep
A rendezvous will keep

# Paper Plates People

Treasures, of life, is found,
in earthen vessels,
Not fine China, but people, like,
in ourselves
Not impressive acts of service
But coming together and converging
Cheap, disposable paper plates never,
underestimate best you could be
It takes us tending needs someone
Never underestimate good you do,
knocking on a door
A real door, phone call, to a friend
You should have shown love more
A scary door be afraid messing up
Knock on it add another win to your cup
Don't worry being find China, looking
sparkling clean sitting on a shelf
Be an earthen jar, that gets dirty,
serving the Lord giving, of yourself

# Morning's First Beam

Dawn pearled the sky
Pillowed on bent arm of
Approaching sunrise
Catches gleam morning's
first beam
Birds whistled and sang
to the dissolving shadows
A sweet song, their silence's
break the sound prolong
Beautiful from all trees
Like harps unseen,
Their arrival upon the scene

# Step Toward Tomorrow

My heart caught in your arms,
love was kept from harm
Memories walked backward,
in footprints in time
Forever sketches in my mind
We, one moment see changes ways,
make the best of our days
Love shimmering gold
Kissed by memories never grows old
Gather up sweetest memories,
in slow drifting song
Guilding deepest faith in love shown
Looked for a place I belong,
then you were there
Seeing love, we both shared
You made me someone more then
a cup half full a beautiful thing
Enriched my heart to sing

# Addressed to My Daughter

Behind curtained eyes I let thoughts,
be uniquely my own
Heart overflowing with love,
in home of sunshine strong
Bothering to ask or notice
my daughter had grown up
Life's sweetest memories in a cup
You're a rainbow day filled sparkling,
treasure after another
Finishing thoughts:
You'll never know how I love you,
because no words described it
If are they're ones I've never learned
Love from the heart chosen to
be heard
I listen all been said, bad or
good sealed them in an envelope of
my heart
Wenda: I wrote upon it love,
where I remembered from the start...

# Paper Town

I wouldn't use one word than,
necessary, to tell my story
Wouldn't waste time with lies tell,
to gain unwanted glory
A day's not a pie, that be cut,
in portions doled in chunks, to suit
our fancy
Hurting others is cruel and nasty
How a strong shot of honesty?
Yet a strong dose of modesty
Emotions are bandaged, not cured,
love can heal
Heartaches and pain are real
Building character comes being
a paper town
Not built upon a rock tumble down…
Not a faithful and useful, is speaking a
smaller truth
Familiar face of dishonesty marks,
evil and shame
As musky rain runs down
a windowpane

# Hush of Winter

Let questions begin:
What thanksgiving answers the
day holds within?
When the sun is waking?
Winter can bring snow and bitterness,
of cold
Leaving a formal expression
All nature's wondrous ways,
One often tried and true confine us,
paint pictures of winter thoughts
Thought that always seem standing by
When with nothing to do
Slowly moving clouds came into view
Spite of everything, gray skies
Will own the day

# Singing Winter's Song

Cute and pretty in ivory white snow,
Winter's the sharpest knife, in the
drawer I know
Christmas's feathery snowflakes
puffed by winds along Christmas's silvery music of
joyful angel's song
Snow glittering like frosted stars
A scene from a postcard, of
winter held so long
Singing the winter's song
Wintry winds; winter's heart
The nudging of sleet, in all a part
Of this glowing testament, to a
happy yuletide memories, to last
When the season's passed

# Sugar and Rose

Every word is a song
To be treasured by your love
Life has been sweet and strong
Time becomes more precious every,
step a dance
I saw love and joy unspeakable,
I caught in a fleeting glance
Your kindness in a rose
When we reach life's end, of
the road
Everything you made complete
A rose by any other would not,
be as sweet
All kindness you've shown me,
I'll do my best to deserve it
Share my earthly journey, of
your spirit
Strong light pushing by darkness,
You are an angel's kiss of light

# Just A Rose

Poetry in the morning sun
Master beauty in each one
And wet from dew
Only a rose will do
A promise of memories to lift,
us on wings of prayer
The rustling Of God's breath,
to kiss each blossom fair
More precious as seasons come
and go
God made them a day's special,
gift When twilight shadows grow
A symbol shows the way we feel
If's love as a seal
All Cod made with such beauty,
had was a rose

# Just One Tear

Before the next tear falls,
You'll be in Heaven
When book of memories of life
Is viewed
Comforts nestle deep in Cod's
love will enfold you
Though many tears have filled
my eyes
They've made the way quite
Clear you're my rainbow in
the sky
To take away the fear
When last my heart's still and
Walk into sunset of my years,
Ill cry joyous tears
One more wondrous glory Ill
look upon your face
Beyond curtains of Heaven's lace

# Funnoy

Life is full of changes
As years come and go
Yet stays the same
My heart bathes in memories that
followed me everywhere I go of
my brother
Memories made knowing each other
He knows the nicest thing to say
I always count on him to help
in understanding way
He's kind and thoughtful and shows,
how he cares
Add goy to my life by being there
Wonderful memories keep me
hanging on
Brings special thanks and love,
that lives on

# Road Home

Happiness a river singing, its
way to the sea
A pleasing sound to me
Gentle memories wash,
over me
Thoughts of home I long to see
Dreamed Of a summer's morn
The world sweet and warm
Home to find a rainbow,
After a rain's storm end
Believe miracles happen since
I was ten
Every mile's a sweet refreshment,
Upon memories stored
Somehow it expresses
Perfect joy comes to mind of happiness

# One's a Lonely Number

If my heart sink despair,
God's there
I'm not a lonely
Other refuge I have none
A voice broke in middle of
a question
According to his word the
smallest prayers are answered
He brought me through the
valleys in my life
All pain and stripe
One's a lonely number, as
you walk life's rugged road
Jesus will lift the heavy road
I'm never alone in His glow
Keep vigil as I go

# A Little Prayer

A new chapter added to,
my life daily,
Healing used each day wisely
Steady trust said a little prayer
Saved forever in heaven's care
Made me find my smile again
find sunshine after the rain
Heart braced the light as I sail
God's light never fails
Much I ought to say
Prayer is my psalm whatever,
the hour
Breathe life into my soul
Gladdens saddest tears,
let sunshine grow

# Peanut Butter Banana Sandwiches

We traded sandwiches, in
the fifth grade,
They were more we could chew
She was best friend I knew
Goodness touching my heart
Sweet thing I remembered,
never deportee
Two sandwiches, one's hers.
the other mine
In my heart kept her memory,
for all time
The angels came for her, she
was only ten
I thought my world had end
Jesus called her with a definite ring
Even I missed her so bad,
Jesus knew an awful
time I had

# Only You Knew

Heart overflows with gratitude
and praise,
Your kindness has followed all
my days
You shine in my eyes, and smile
in my heart
A slow, unhurried little smile
tugged in position, from
the start
Prayer heard; laughter learned
sewed love in my heart
Closing big hole of pain
Found sunshine in the rain made
thing important to you and me
Flowers blooms because of you
Morning sweet after the dew
Sweet evening decorated with happiness
Ransomed all your goodness
Fill my heart of joy and song;
As heard an echo
My heard was too timid to let you know

# Rose Of Sharon

Upon a sheet of paper I wrote,
my thoughts mingle with
Yesterday revealed the past; today tells
another passing year
Thoughts of a rose each petal feels, like
silk clothes of gentleness, touch Of
her kindness
Kindly words prove a friend Indeed,
mercy, softly breathed
Softly answers turn away the pain, finds.
sunshine after the rain
Her memory becomes more precious, as days
come and go
Each dawning morning a special gift when
twilight shadows grow
Sweet memories pressed under an angel's wing
Kept In light of eternity

# Secret of Spring

Eating up attention is spring
Next a little bind resting in
a nest begins to Sing
Sun took step farther and shone
gleaming like a new penny
Geese in V-formation across the
sky was many
A gentle breeze touched lovely flowers
Clad in pink and white danced from
the recent showers
Everything so grand; lovely pattern
hand-in hand
Still Impressed played host with,
spring's heart
A mirrored vision brought forward
by coming Of March

# Whispering Wings

In shadows of wings cause It's,
wonderful to have something to
believe in
Precious time reflect upon when
I'll see you again
Wings In the morning designed to
be by my Side
I felt you comforting me arms
out so wide
Sweet memories standing by to dry
each tear I cry in tender heart away;
I know I'll see you someday
Knowing is uplifting when lonely
Who gladdens up my heart,
but you only?
I may not see their wings, yet
ceremoniously caressed my heart
Declare Innocent eagerness share,
My journey as long March

# Hands of March

Sweetness Of the day cupped
around me
It had a schedule I was to see
Of an antique blue sky slowly
Moving clouds of imitation lace,
reflected in a pond nearby
Lemon pale light of sun
Message of cheer
So gentle in arms of tender rain,
rainbow stayed near
Tokens another day come again
Symbol promise of hope and
dreams to pain
One impression awesome to see
It's useless to attempt to tell,
the wonders to try
Day of pearls and golden sunshine
These toted loses to succeed in
cherish lifetimes

# Catch 22

Spring hides herself no one see
Plans and dreams what yet to be
Finger Of light pulled down. It's honey rays,
Falls on a butterfly it had found
In a cherish shine Catch 22
Equal meaning of sweet and
pure persuasion
22 situations
Started me a bit enough to
sharpen me
Captured more casuals to see
She Is of the sky, and cherished
by the wind
Knows to use talents and when
A perfect breeze loves her still,
Coaxing flights with kisses of
the air
Summoned rain to kiss each
flower blossoms fair
She speaks with a small truth
caught in a Catch 22

# Woods and Templed Hills

This tender, quiet morning gentleness, was
something new
A pretty quiet morning, when pleasures,
are few
The imminence down, woods and templed
hills made sun seeking top canopy able
to reach
Transformed, by radiance walk. on in peace
Shine on rocks and rills
Woods and templed hills
My heart with rapture thrills
One heartfelt sentence, brilliantly summarized
what It's all about
Let the rocks with their silence break,
Walk onward never doubt
As walking, by a friend on I depend
One serves a purpose, to console, and
encourage me

# Music Received the Breeze

Dawn pearled the sky
Cheeks pillowed on the ben arm of
the approaching sunrise
Now it catches the gleam of the
morning first beam
Birds whistled and sang to the
dissolving shadows
Sweet is the song when their
silence breaks and sound prolong
The music receives the breeze
Swelled ringing from all the trees
Beautiful music, from heavenly
angel's harps unseen
Countless ages anxiously,
we united their arrival, upon the scene

# Laughing in Time with Midnight Whispers

Under thoughts between silence,
laughing time with midnight:
Whispers, is a soft rustling sound
Channel of peace touched down
With whispered words walked in
stayed that night
Where baby stars, moon and
clouds take Right
Like creamy chocolate elusive,
ministered of the night
Fed a soul running freely with
peace so sweet
Sweetness of a rose lay at my feet
Midnight sky sparkled like diamonds
sort of a spur, of a moment decision
In time settling, on high commission
The moon squatting down in a
corner of the sky to Sleep
Succumbed in edifice's peace

# Top of the Day

All-purpose day, no trace, of
dark clouds
The little rest in her homeplace
Nothing to conceal. except clouds,
tuck inside blue skies
The Sun plea her yearning cries
her sunlight not, to be lost, to lose
a chance shares the cost
Little birds looked for any kind, of an
excuse to sing
And feeling of total freedom, purpose;
for things
Mothering winds brought a rose
scented breeze
Elected when butterflies and bees,
float free
All together pressured info jewels.
shine so bright
One perfect day felt right

# The Rose

Brace each rose
With thoughts, of someone dear
Whom love commits you here
Immerse the rose
With feelings of love, to and from,
a beginning passes
standing in present above
It grows and becomes stronger
as use got Older
And proves its solid gold
Let love become a spark of dreams
A little singing sparkling stream
Give your heart to her
This moment made to last
Follows days, Of the past
Love and happiness
Working their way in
These are needed you to win

# Priceless Flower

Many a voice will greet us,
a low and gentle tone
Its music will not Cheer us
Like the cadence of your Own
You brought 10,000 sunsets, of
friendly smiles to us
Jeweled nets of violets when
your love was deeded us
Ten thousand dewy mornings
A mossy glade with willow shade:
music on spring
wild rose rambling free
A meadow starred with flowers,
you loved so:
A priceless love… sewed.

# Teardrops and Hearts

There are, it may be.
Lifetime Of losses with no
mourning allowed
Aching wounds left forever unhealed
Shadows Of thoughts run deep
Many questions no answer to keep
Intertwine my mind
Helped open this heart of mine
Put two paper teardrops together,
Made little heart for you
Gift of love I knew.
Anytime I take a tea. made something.
positive help you forget
The pain caused it
You'll never shed a tear... again
Here till then... life does last
forgetting the past
All I see now...

# Memories Sweetly Sleep

Ink Rows the beauty of the word
Feelings form on paper
Coming together, then
separating once again
Hours of early morn
Thoughts Of you come softly
Never becoming time worn
Sleeping Beauty -the light
enveloping you
Forming shapes like musical notes;
loving words reaching, in to bring
you here
Memories sweet
Difficulties to leave, impossible to forget
Memories flutes, no regrets
I leave my paper on the table
and pencil beside It
Going back as sleep comes once again

# No Crystal China Nice

Words Of praise leaves you
Befuddled and tippy as a mouse
Annoyed when roused
Dream emotions to drink from
Hose the gala with exceptional aplomb
A test you don't have, to study,
to pass
Just accept the lessons that will,
no doubt last
Despite the odds
Don't try to cheat
That way you could not be weak
Not crystal China nice
Try hard you'll find
Yourself in a winning streak twice

# Goodbye

As I walk the step into the sky
I realize I never said goodbye
Flowers rise to kiss each day
You always gave me a treasured
smile way
The day was made new the day was old
Dreams of gold
Stir up in remembrance
You once said:
When I am gone, release me,
let me go
I have many things to see
and do
You mustn't tie yourself to
me with tears
Be happy that we had many years
Yes, I remember I really do
Now the time to say goodbye
to you

# October Coloring Book

October has a sense of color
A fondness for details
Nimble fingers creating pretty
touches to your day
In a majestic way
Aura Of dawn stained the eastern
sky, in deep rose color
Wise combine with each other
Carved silver ribbons, from,
clouds of mist
Caught the eye of a Novelist
Hazy shades of pink slipped Into
washed blue dawn
Sandaled feet upon the lawn
Mysterious beauty-victory cry,
of sunrise
Announces its capture of the day

# Tear–Stained Heart

Nothing speaks to the soul,
like our despair
Leaving to question, are we
truly prepare?
A tear so small carries much emotions
Grievance comes Out portion
We need not worry, nor should we fear
I hear no footsteps at my side
But know God's with me abide
I felt his light
My feelings stirred
His light will guide me
His love he allowed me to see

# Whispered Words

Sensual September morning,
secretly happen by
Suddenly, unannounced,
whirling with emotions,
Humming... with whispered,
words of a love-sweet song
September celebrating
love evensong
Mystical morning
Rendezvous out of season,
warming hearts, calmly…
embracing love -
With whispered words,
of love
Lost in Autumntime
Casually... quickly
And in rhyme
Whispered vow-solemn,
promise endows

# Love You

Our heart was cushioned
on heart-felt warmth
Nourished with spoonful,
of love
Shines in dreadful weather
Our heart was cushioned on,
heart-felt warmth
We need not a hearth
Our love Is cushioned on
winning smiles
Shines as a beacon
Every day and night
Not need a brightener
Is cushioned on friendly,
love habits
Nurtured with respect
Don't need a softener

# Life's many Pages

One side leaf of paper existed,
through ages
Pressed between beginning end
Place where something one began
Pages Of time unfold been folded,
take hold
Memories a chapter, in a book
Covers we can quickly look
Each ensuing a page, has a
different photo
Every page, there are mementos
Nurture the tenderest phrase
Champion Of verse…
Names, dates, of children
and grandchildren
History, of times past, a gentle,
Reminder, all good times won't last

# A Walk-Through Winter

A journey to spring
A wild rose rambling tree
Our dance floor the moon,
our spotlight
Stream of pearls, waterfall,
nest of velvet tears
Hemmed in satin ribbons of
stars over the years
Like a world of glass
Rich in a cold brass
Shadow dance in the moonlight,
as hues of grey across the sky,
Sigh in almost small retreats,
fails in vast defeat
Colors begin to drift away
To this marvelous day

# What A Day

Haven't had a day, this
such a long time
Floors should, be vacuumed,
dishes put away
Clothes are piled up, I'm too
fatigued to try
I'd better mow the grass, but
hard getting dress
Should stayed, in bed and get,
mu rest
To be lazy, is it such a crime?
I haven't had a day this such,
A long time

# Summer Blue

Clutching a rainbow of
balloons, in her hand
Mighty, in strength and
Obedient to every command
Was caught up in endless time
To ascend gradually make the climb
The has dimmed to Autumn's hues,
burning gold in view
Falling leaves and shorter days,
soon gilled into Winter's ways
Seasons held onto her, to see
But winter came, to set her free
Sunshine's here but hidden
It will take some time to ridden

# Flight of the Dove

End of a day, as curtain of
dusk begins to fall
I heard a dove softly call
At morning down afternoon
became sunbeams shining down
Her song reminded me of summer
seasons and evening at dusk
Changing to nighttime dreams
peaceful tranquility it leaves
For the little dove standing by,
rushes my heart to dry, each
tear I cry
On wings of a dove… with a
message of love
Delivering in a tender,
heartfelt way
It's special and glorious Of
brightening my day

# Indian Summer

Transformed by radiance of
golden light
To bathe her beauty there
Come radiant and fair
In sweet colors, of delight
In a waving veil
Under a sky so pale
The clouds seemed caught up
In Mother of Pearls combs
While in steps
Parting the azure shroud
Placing her foot, into a scarlet
pretty cloud
A beautiful day of dawn
Quickly gold-leafed meadows,
and lawns

# Grandpa's Clock

In my head standing carved,
in memories forever
A small piece of heaven
bonded together
Like finding a flower
I could see without my eyes
And something deep within me
heard last silent cries
Grandpa's clock has been
through times
Deep as church bell's chimes
My memories of tenderness,
given tone
Seeking them strong in
My heart where it belongs

# Yellow Ribbon

Sometimes I laugh I feel guilty
For a moment I've forgotten
Then I remember the sound of your laughter
And I eye mist:
Life is, and be no other way a twist
A yellow ribbon is a symbol
of sorrow
Throughout today and tomorrow
You are a sailor. Faith In oneself -
Honor- To principle
Loyalty to the cause of good news,
bind to evil
Integrity - In face of adversity
honestly all you do
Proud- All fifty bright stars.
On our flag
Always hoped served your country
Meant freedom have a champion
Many missing in action some names,
You can't recall
I pray you'll not just another hero
Added to the list on a wall

# Poem of the Morning

In early morn all slumbering,
in dreams
there Is One awake
writing, by moonbeams…
A poem comes to me so clear
Letting the world know the
inner feelings, so dear Tripping across the paper and
scamper through my mind,,.
Not a thing can stop the words
My heart does find
Words gentle combined in one
sentence who read to see

# Prissy

Had a dog stubborn as a mule
But wasn't a fool
Thought call her sissy, but
found character of that dog
Her personality was mild and shy as fog
Took her to the park to play,
alone and run on her own
She was so funny: way she
walked with a swing
That changed everything
Sissy became Prissy
The name suited her best all
the rest
A perfect name ever could be,
how she twisted you see

# Winter Ice

By the cracking fire faint,
moaning, of the wind.
Tops Of the trees Creaked-in
the wind
As though talking to each other,
up there
Branches no longer stay-still
And bow down- in reverence, to the
Change in the air
A cold icy winter night
All is still dresses in white
The sky beaded in crystal stars.
Like diamonds scattered, from a
silver cup
A shining crescent moon rises
slowly up
And wearing a crystal crown
And papery gown

# About the Author

Get to know me, you'll feel you've known me a lifetime. My Poetry is warm and charming. Experience a slower, gently way of life. Uncover layers of writing. I stay involved with family friends. I am involved in everything around me.

www.ingramcontent.com/pod-product-compliance
Lightning Source LLC
Chambersburg PA
CBHW020344130626
46549CB00003B/1284